MW00461289

PHARMACOPOEIA

PHARMACOPOEIA

A DUNGENESS NOTEBOOK

VINTAGE CLASSICS
LONDON

5 7 9 10 8 6

Vintage Classics is part of the Penguin Random House group of companies
whose addresses can be found at global.penguinrandomhouse.com

Extracts from *Modern Nature* Copyright © The Keith Collins Will Trust,
Derek Jarman 1991
Extracts from *Smiling in Slow Motion* Copyright © The Keith Collins Will Trust,
Derek Jarman 2000
Extracts from *Chroma* Copyright © The Keith Collins Will Trust,
Derek Jarman 1994
Extracts from *Derek Jarman's Garden* Copyright © The Keith Collins Will Trust,
Derek Jarman 1995
Foreword © Tilda Swinton 2020, 2022

Derek Jarman has asserted his right to be identified as the author of this Work in
accordance with the Copyright, Designs and Patents Act 1988

First published in Great Britain by Vintage Classics in 2022

penguin.co.uk/vintage-classics

A CIP catalogue record for this book is available from the British Library

ISBN 9781784877330

Typeset in 11/18pt Dante MT Pro by Jouve (UK), Milton Keynes
Printed and bound in China by C&C Offset Printing Co., Ltd.

The authorised representative in the EEA is Penguin Random House Ireland,
Morrison Chambers, 32 Nassau Street, Dublin D02 YH68

Penguin Random House is committed to a sustainable future
for our business, our readers and our planet. This book is made
from Forest Stewardship Council® certified paper.

EDITOR'S NOTE

This book is composed of extracts from across Derek Jarman's published works. In particular, it draws upon his journals, *Modern Nature* and *Smiling in Slow Motion*, his ode to colour, *Chroma*, and the posthumously published, *Derek Jarman's Garden*. *Pharmacopoeia* was conceived as a celebration of Derek Jarman's nature writing and was begun with the approval of Keith Collins and the Keith Collins Will Trust.

FOREWORD

Artists live in houses and make work in them; they make work in other people's houses, too. There are countless plaques on countless walls across the globe running to catch up with the trail of inspired moments down the ages: 'here he wrote such and such', 'between the years blank and blank, she completed so and so', 'he lived here', 'she boarded here', even 'for a week/a night, they slept here'. Artists also work on the bus, in trains, in cafes and on the sides of roads, under trees and canvas and bed-clothes by torchlight. Let's maybe conclude that art is generated everywhere.

This idea flicks a beautiful switch, in my view. It de-exoticises and brings closer the idea of an artist's work, rubs it into the landscape of regular – lived – human life. This is closer to an accurate picture, as I know it to be. Artists – writers, painters, sculptors, film-makers, perform-ers, musicians, philosophers – make work within our lived days and in between the doorways of a social mortal span . . . It would be impossible to catch, therefore, like a butterfly in a net, every site of every artist's creative inspiration. Let's just say that might be The World Itself, after all.

But there are some places that represent something worth preserving – not, in fact, simply because they represent a past point in history and a footnote regarding a single life once lived, but because of the influence they had on that life, the working practice they made possible, the liminal energy they afforded and might still afford open souls seeking their nourishment.

I first saw Prospect Cottage the day that Derek did. We had driven down to find a bluebell wood to shoot in: I had remembered a wide bluebell expanse in Kent from my schooldays there. We pottered down in my ramshackle little car and found the idyll now covered in concrete. A little disheartened, we headed for the coast, abandoning bluebells in search of fresh air. Derek's father had recently died and left him a small inheritance. Life on Charing Cross Road had become somewhat overstimulating, and Derek was looking for a place to be quieter. He had a friend who lived on the shingle at Dungeness, that pocket of southern England which sounded to me so tantalisingly Scottish, the 'dangerous nose', the Fifth Quarter of the globe . . .

We drove along the shore road and stopped to skim flat

stones like flints into the waves, pocket a few pebbles that we found with perfect holes in them, little knowing that this would be the first of a thousand afternoons for us spent in much the same way. As we were turning to drive back to London, we saw, at the same moment, a small black-painted wooden house with yolk-yellow window frames on the left-hand side of the road facing the sea. It had a For Sale sign stuck in the stones at its feet. I remember distinctly turning in without a word and stopping the car.

We knocked on the door, were let in by the charming lady who lived there and, after a tour that cannot have lasted longer than fifteen minutes, were back on the road heading north. Derek decided before we reached Lydd that he would buy it. And within a couple of months, we were taking down chintz curtains and prising open the lid of the first of gazillion gallons of pitch-black paint with which to anoint his new kingdom.

The pleasure he took in transforming this modest bungalow into the Tardis he created – the setting for his films, his books, his garden, the solace of the sea and the peculiar glamour of the nuclear power station (!) – especially at the moment at which he discovered himself ill . . . is incalculable. He made of this wee house, his wooden tent pitched in the wilderness, an artwork – and out of its shingle skirts, an ingenious garden – now internationally recognised. But, first and foremost, the cottage was always a living thing, a practical toolbox for his work.

Our initiative to preserve this treasure that might otherwise be lost to our cultural landscape is not that we are seeking to set in a time warp a precious object of historical significance for posterity only; but, crucially, to resuscitate and ensure the continued vibrational existence of a living battery: to clear space around it and feed the energy of a resource that was only ever intended to be that. This is a vision not of taking but of giving.

Just as Derek was self-determinedly dedicated to process above product, to collective work, to empowering voices that might feel alienated, my excitement about this vision for Prospect Cottage lives in its projected future as an open, inclusive and encouraging machine for the inspiration and functional working lives of those who might come and share in its special qualities, qualities that, as a young artist, I was lucky enough to benefit from alongside Derek and so many of our friends and fellow travellers.

Beyond the plaques, there are some places that offer the vision of a continued evolution as a point of encouragement and metaphysical enlightenment. I suggest that Prospect Cottage is such a place.

Derek – memorably – said that he would prefer his works after his death to evaporate and disappear. For what it's worth, and in honour of the supremely contrary nature of my friend, I feel fully confident that he would be extremely enthusiastic about the generosity of this vision for the continuance of the life of his beloved Prospect Cottage as a possibility for future artists, thinkers, activists, gardeners to gain from it the practical and spiritual nourishment it lent him and for which he was – and is – eternally grateful . . .

Tilda Swinton

2020

PHARMACOPOEIA

to whom it may concern

in the dead stones of a planet

no longer remembered as earth

may he decipher this opaque hieroglyph

perform an archaeology of soul

on these precious fragments

all that remains of our vanished days

here – at the sea's edge

I have planted a stony garden

dragon tooth dolmen spring up

to defend the porch

steadfast warriors

GORSE & GOLD

I live in borrowed time, therefore I see no reason in the world why my heart grows not dark.

A cold wind blows tonight over this desolate island.

Over the hills and dales, over mountain and marsh, down the great roads and little lanes, through the villages and small towns, through the great towns and the cities.

Everywhere it blows through empty streets and desolate houses, rattling the hedgerows and broken windows, drumming on locked doors.

This wind is blowing high in the tower blocks and steeples, down along the river, invading houses and mansions, through the corridors and up the staircases, rustling the faded curtains in bedrooms, over the carpets, up the aisles and down in the crypts, in public places and private, among forgotten secrets, round the armchair, the easy chair, across the kitchen table.

So icy is this wind that it rattles the bones in the graves and sends rats shivering down the sewers.

Fragments of memory eddy past and are lost in the dark. In the gusts yellowing half-forgotten papers whirl old headlines up and over dingy suburban houses, past leaders and obituaries, the debris of inaction, into the void. Thought illuminated briefly by lightning. The rainbows are put out, the crocks of gold lie rusting – forgotten as the fallen trees which strew the fields and dead meadows.

I consider the lives of warriors, how they suddenly left their halls.

Bold and noble leaders,
I shiver and regret my time.

But the wind does not stop for my thoughts. It whips across the flooded gravel pits drumming up waves on their waters that glint hard and metallic in the night, over the shingle, rustling the dead gorse and skeletal bugloss, running in rivulets through the parched grass – while I sit here in the dark holding a candle that throws my divided shadow across the room, and gathers my thoughts to the flame like moths.

I have not moved for many hours. Years, a lifetime, eddy past: one, two, three: into the small hours, the clock chimes. The wind is singing now.

Eternity, eternity
Where will you spend eternity?
Heaven or hell, which shall it be,
Where will you spend eternity?

And then the wind is gone, chasing itself across the shingle to lose itself in the waves which brush past the Ness, throwing up plumes of salt spray which spatter across the windows. Nothing can hide from it. Certainly no man can be wise before he has lived his share of winters in the world.

The wind calls my name, Prophesy.

Long past the creator destroyed this earth, the joyful songs of the people were silent, the ancient works of giants stood desolate.

The wind whirls in the gutters, screams in the telegraph poles.

I'll huff and I'll puff,
And I'll blow your house down.

Time is scattered, the past and the future, the future past and present. Whole lives are erased from the book by the great dictator, the screech of the pen across the page, your name, Prophesy, your name! The wind circles the empty hearth casting a pall of dust, the candle fizzes. Who called this up? Did I?

Now throughout the world stand windblown halls, frost-covered ruined buildings; the wine halls crumble, kings lie dead, deprived of pleasure, all the steadfast band dead by the wall.

The storm blew itself out by two – before returning at four with a sudden blast, illuminated by one brilliant lightning flash, and no thunder.

The foghorn sounded for half an hour and then all went quiet.

Buffeted in my sleep like a boat in a high sea, I never cross the night without waking. I can't quite remember when it was different. I slept quite soundly for forty years; then something changed. Perhaps I wake myself in case I die, unconscious, at the low ebb of the night. Bergman's hour of the wolf.

The next day I can't remember what passed through my mind. Nothing, perhaps, except a vague unease.

It's cold tonight; but suddenly I'm up and pissing in the dark. Back in bed the pillows have been pummelled into uncomfortable hillocks, the sheets have parted company with the mattress – I doze off.

In the morning the storm has torn up a mountain of kelp which floats back and forth in the foam at the sea's edge. The wind is up again, seagulls float ever closer as if I gave off some imperceptible warmth in the cold. I beat the tide which is racing in, and find three stones for the new flower bed. I draw the circle to plant them but retire inside as the rain blows in; settle down at my desk for a cold wet day.

Prospect Cottage, its timbers black with pitch, stands on the shingle at Dungeness. Built eighty years ago at the sea's edge – one stormy night many years ago waves roared up to the front door threatening to swallow it . . . Now the sea has retreated leaving bands of shingle. You can see these clearly from the air; they fan out from the lighthouse at the tip of the Ness like contours on a map.

Prospect faces the rising sun across a road sparkling silver with sea mist. One small clump of dark green broom breaks through the flat ochre shingle. Beyond, at the sea's edge, are silhouetted a jumble of huts and fishing boats, and a brick kutch, long abandoned, which has sunk like a pillbox at a crazy angle; in it, many years ago, the fishermen's nets were boiled in amber preservative.

There are no walls or fences. My garden's boundaries are the horizon. In this desolate landscape the silence is only broken by the wind, and the gulls squabbling round the fishermen bringing in the afternoon catch.

There is more sunlight here than anywhere in Britain; this and the constant wind turn the shingle into a stony desert where only the toughest grasses take a hold – paving the way for sage-green sea kale, blue bugloss, red poppy, yellow sedum.

The shingle is home to larks. In the spring I've counted as many as a dozen singing high above, lost in a blue sky. Flocks of greenfinches wheel past in spirals, caught in a scurrying breeze. At low tide the sea rolls back to reveal a wide sandbank, on which seabirds vanish like quicksilver as they fly close to the ground. Gulls feed alongside fishermen digging lug. When a winter storm blows up, cormorants skim the waves that roar along the Ness – throwing stones pell-mell along the steep bank.

The view from my kitchen at the back of the house is bounded to the left by the old Dungeness lighthouse, and the iron grey bulk of the nuclear reactor – in front of which dark green broom and gorse, bright with yellow flowers, have formed little islands in the shingle, ending in a scrubby copse of sallow and ash dwarfed and blasted by the gales.

In the middle of the copse is a barren pear tree that has struggled for a century to reach ten feet; underneath this a carpet of violets. Gnarled dog roses guard this secret spot – where on a calm summer day meadow browns and blues congregate in their hundreds, floating past the spires of nettles thick with black tortoiseshell caterpillars.

High above a lone hawk hovers, while far away on the blue horizon the tall medieval tower of Lydd church, the cathedral of the marshes, comes and goes in a heat haze.

My sense of confusion has come to a head, catalysed by my public announcement of the HIV infection. Now I no longer know where the focus is, for myself, or in the minds of my audience. Reaction to me has changed.

There is an element of worship, which worries me. Perhaps I courted it.

In any case I had no choice, I've always hated secrets, the canker that destroys; better out in the daylight and be done with it. But if only it were that easy – my whole being has changed; my wild nights on the vodka are now only an aggravating memory, an itch before turning in. Two years have passed with a few desultory nights out. Even with safer sex I've felt the life of my partner was in my hands. Hardly the cue for a night of abandonment. I've come a long way in accepting the restraint. But I dream of an unlikely old age as a hairy satyr.

This lament is not borne out by my state of mind; because apart from the nagging past – film, sex and

London – I have never been happier than last week. I look up and see the deep azure sea outside my window in the February sun, and today I saw my first bumble bee. Planted lavender and clumps of red-hot poker.

I waited a lifetime to build my garden,
I built my garden with the colours of healing,
On the sepia shingle at Dungeness.
I planted a rose and then an elder,
Lavender, sage, and Crambe maritima,
Lovage, parsley, santolina,
Hore hound, fennel, mint and rue.
Here was a garden to soothe the mind,
A garden of circles and wooden henges,
Circles of stone, and sea defences.
And then I added the rust brown scrap,
A float, a malin and old tank trap.
Dig in your soul with the compost from Lydd,
Cuttings, divisions are placed in frames,
Protected from rabbits with neat wood cones.
My garden sings with the winds in winter.
Braving the salt which sails in plumes,
From the rolling breakers that gnaw the shingle.

No Hortus Conclusus, my seaside garden.
With poet's sleeping and dreaming of daisies.
I'm wide awake on this Sunday morning.
All the colours are present in this new garden.
Purple iris, imperial sceptre;
Green of the buds breaking on elder;
Browns of the humus, and ochre grasses;
Yellows in August on Helichrysum,
That turns in September to orange and brown;
Blue of the bugloss, and self-sown cornflower;
Blue of the sage and winter hyacinth;
Pink and white roses blowing in June;
And the scarlet rosehips, fiery in winter;
The bitter sloes to make sweet gin.
Brambles in autumn,
And gorse in the spring.

For two months after moving here I spent hours each day picking up fragments of countless smashed bottles, china plates, pieces of rusty metal. There was a bike, cooking pots, even an old bedstead. Rubbish had been scattered over the whole landscape. Each day I thought I had got to the end of the task only to find the shingle had thrown up another crop overnight.

Sunny days were the best for clearing up, as the glass and pottery glinted. I buried the lot on the site of an old bonfire at the bottom of the garden in a large mound, which I covered with the clumps of grass I dug out when I built the shingle garden.

This landscape without visible boundaries is yet jealous of its privacy. Wandering across it, unhindered by fence or hedge, you stumble across piles of rubbish. Maybe that old car still belongs to someone. Who owns the corrugated hut blown sideways at the seashore? Its workbench is strewn with pots of rusting nails, spanners, rasps, an old vice, anchors, and coils of wire – a haven for ghostly ancestors to shelter from a brutish December easterly.

Time and tide have shipwrecked a huge tree, whose gnarled roots, bleached and bony, still grasp the rocks torn up with it. Who sat on those old canvas chairs, warped by the passing seasons, carefully placed alongside each other waiting for their owner's return?

I walk along the seashore each day, and it guards its secrets. Who plunged these anchors into their shingly graves? This rusting shadow on the ground was once somebody's bed. Old winches and hawsers, graves of toil and memories of angry seas – dissolving.

The rain and fine warm weather have quickened the landscape – brought the saturated spring colours early. The dead of winter is passed. Today Dungeness glowed under a pewter sky – shimmering emeralds, arsenic, sap, sage and verdigris greens washed bright, moss in little islands set off against pink pebbles, glowing yellow banks of gorse, the deep russet of dead bracken, and pale ochre of reeds in clumps set against the willow spinney – a deep burgundy, with silvery catkins and fans of ochre yellow stamens fringed with the slightest hint of lime green of newly burst leaves.

This symphony of colour I have seen in no other landscape. Dungeness is a premonition of the far North, a landscape Southerners might think drear and monotonous, which sings like the birch woods in Sibelius' music.

From my home I can see the sun clamber out of a misty sea. It wakes me through the bedroom window and then stays with me all day. There are no trees or hills to hide it. When it sets over the flatlands in the west I sit and watch it on a throne-like chair that I rescued from a rubbish dump. I never miss the setting sun, however cold the weather.

Tonight it hangs huge and scarlet after a day of dark clouds. It appears for a few brief minutes, a perfect circle before disappearing – then the darkness comes rushing across the sky to embrace the inky timbers of Prospect Cottage; but before the light is extinguished the house reflects gold, or, as this evening, blazes ruby, its panes of glass a dazzling scarlet. At this moment so red is the light all the greens turn black as pitch, the gorse and broom like jet-black sea anemones, a vast and sombre silhouette.

The heavy rain has left sheets of water reflecting the grey sky lying on the sharp green of the spring fields. All along the rail embankment to Ashford the buds are breaking on the hawthorn bushes. There are drifts of primroses everywhere.

It's a cold windy day; a drizzle blankets the view, stinging the eyes. Nevertheless a week's absence has brought the garden on. A quick look showed the irises have grown inches and a second helping of daffodils are unfolding in the broom. The roses are all in bud and are coping with the cold winds.

At the end of the garden the dwarf sloe bushes have blossomed; and the woods along the Long Pits shimmer with silver pussy willow. The Pits are two flooded gravel quarries – there is a pumping station in case anything goes wrong with the nuclear power station's cooling system.

Deep in the middle of the woods, in the most secret glade, primroses are blooming, the only ones I have found; but there are carpets of violets almost hidden by their bright green leaves.

The unobservant could walk by them without noticing as the leaves and flowers create an almost perfect camouflage, the elusive purple vanishing in the green.

As a nine-year-old on the cliffs at Hordle I discovered a bank of sweet violets and used to creep through the hedge that enclosed the school playing field and lie in the sun dreaming. What did I dream in my violet youth?

The violet held a secret.

Along the hedgerow that ran down to the cliffs at Hordle deep purple violets grew – perhaps no more than a dozen plants. I stumbled across them late one sunny March afternoon as I came up the cliff path from the sea. They were hidden in a small recess. I stood for some moments dazzled by them.

Day after day I returned from the dull regimental existence of an English boarding school to my secret garden – the first of many that blossomed in my dreams. It was here that I brought him, sworn to secrecy, and then watched him slip out of his grey flannel suit and lie naked in the spring sunlight. Here our hands first touched; then I pulled down my trousers and lay beside him. Bliss that he turned and lay naked on his stomach, laughing as my hand ran down his back and disappeared into the warm darkness between his thighs. He called it 'the lovely feeling' and returned the next day, inviting me into his bed that night.

Obsessive violets drawing the evening shadows to themselves, our fingers touching in the purple.

Term ended. I bought myself violets from the florist's and put them by my bedside. My grandmother disapproved of flowers in the bedroom, said they corrupted the air. Violets, she said, were the flower of death.

But the violet, I discovered, was third in the trinity of symbolic flowers, flower of purity,

Whose virtue neither the heat of the sun melted away,
Neither the rain has washed and driven away.

The violet, *Nothing behind the best for smelling sweetly, a thousand more will provoke your content.*

A new orchard and garden was mine.

That summer, when the wheat had grown waist high,

we carved a secret path from the violet grove into the centre of the field, and lay there chewing the unformed seeds, rubbing ourselves all over each other's bronzed and salty bodies, such was our happy garden state.

The wind roared through the night with but brief moments of calm – early this morning the whole landscape, sea and sky blended into a glowering ochre – even the lark's song was blown away. My roses are now sadly scorched and the fennel quite dead.

In the house the seeds sprout: Californian poppy, pennyroyal and chives have germinated. This afternoon a misty sun gave some respite but was quickly drawn behind a grey gloom that loomed out of the west.

At tea I walked a mile along the shore, skirting heavy leaden waves. Returned home tired, breathless and drenched with salt. Tracking back I noticed dandelions and dead-nettles growing in the shadow of a broken-backed fisherman's hut. The pitch-black timbers of Prospect Cottage, with its bright yellow windows, are silhouetted against banks of gorse ablaze with golden flowers.

When I came to Dungeness in the mid-eighties, I had no thought of building a garden. It looked impossible: shingle with no soil supported a sparse vegetation. Outside the front door a bed had been built – a rockery of broken bricks and concrete: it fitted well. One day, walking on the beach at low tide, I noticed a magnificent flint. I brought it back and pulled out one of the bricks. Soon I had replaced all the rubble with flints. They were hard to find, but after a storm a few more would appear. The bed looked great, like dragon's teeth – white and grey. My journey to the sea each morning had purpose.

I decided to stop there; after all, the bleakness of Prospect Cottage was what had made me fall in love with it. At the back I planted a dog rose. Then I found a curious piece of driftwood and used this, and one of the necklaces of holey stones on the wall, to stake the rose.

The garden had begun.

I saw it as a therapy and a pharmacopoeia.

Grey, cool morning, the ochre shingle and sea that is swallowed in the mist. I'm having difficulty eating, everything tastes terrible. I was sick in the night but slept like a log, up just before six. I'm very weak as I had no supper last night.

I love this grey weather – the sunlight attacks me. With my gold pen, the little diary, Mr Wobble. I've made myself a bowl of porridge and eaten an orange. The garden welcomes the day. An exquisite tulip, red and yellow and frilly, has popped up in the wallflowers, which are spectacular this year.

I walked down to the sea, my stomach rumbling like the machine-gun fire on Lydd range. A wide expanse of sand, deserted except for two men catching shrimp and another digging for lug. It's wonderful, a day alone, looking after myself quite successfully.

The rain wept through the night, quietened the grumbling shingle, stilled me into sleep. In the distance the sea roared, churning the ochrous sandbanks. The shoreline had changed, as if a giant hand had raked the shingle, smoothing out the small coves, grading the dips and hollows into a perfect straight line. At the base of the bank a fast-moving river had formed. No stones were left to build the mazes and labyrinths of my garden.

The rain fell through the small hours. Dreamt of soldiers: I was reluctant to wear the smart uniform. The handsomest I glimpsed high above me on the scaffolding around some marble ruin. Stopped, held my breath for his beauty. He slipped out of his uniform and, carefully folding it, placed it at the foot of my bed. A rush of cool air as he slid beneath the sheets. He dared not wake me as he knew I would disappear – I was his dream.

My elder tree died in the night, burnt black by the salt spray . . .

Bour tree, bour tree, crooked rong
Never straight and never strong
Ever bush and never tree
Since our Lord was nailed on thee

A great pool of water formed on the path, so that as he left the traveller saw his face reflected. He smiled and called back.

The day started with two brief showers. A cold breeze, but the sun came back, and stayed. Driving to Rye we noticed banks of alexanders, bright green with creamy yellow flowers, at the kerbside. At the gravel pits we counted a flock of over thirty swans grazing amongst the sheep.

All the way the gardens were bright with spring flowers, particularly marigolds, which run riot . . .

Back home I walked along the deserted beach past the power station. The west side of the Ness has a different vegetation. It's flat. There are patches of moss, islands of dead broom, thrift and an abundance of foxgloves. At the sea's edge there is horned poppy, but little if any sea kale.

Further past the pylons there is a golden island of gorse. Here, even in the cold wind, the air is scented. Gorse has a delicate herbal perfume not unlike rue. In the right weather conditions the whole Ness smells of it.

There is a passage into the largest clump, a huge area a

hundred yards or more in diameter; deep inside, a golden light and a heady perfume. The bushes seem ancient – serpentine gnarled trunks, as if wrung ferociously in an easterly gale. Many of them, long dead, form a carpet like a writhing snake pit.

The great bushes are about ten feet high, very luxuriant, and the warm winter has produced the most beautiful blossom.

This evening the silence in this grove was truly golden. It is a beautiful thought that Pliny says gorse was used to catch the specks of gold from the gravel that prospectors panned.

The gardener digs in another time, without past or future, beginning or end. A time that does not cleave the day with rush hours, lunch breaks, the last bus home. As you walk in the garden you pass into this time – the moment of entering can never be remembered. Around you the landscape lies transfigured. Here is the Amen beyond the prayer.

Dante, at the beginning of his journey back along the great antique spiral, entered this realm in a dark wood.

Nel mezzo del cammin di nostra vita
Mi ritrovai per una selva oscura
Ché la diritta via era smarrita

A hallucinatory dusk, washed with colours to drive Monet to suicide. At sunset the brightest sickle moon appeared in a gentle blue sky; minute by minute gathering in intensity it stayed until just before midnight.

Night clear as a bell – the blue passed through violet with strands of rose and old gold to become a deep indigo. So etched were the moon and stars they seemed to have been cut out by a child to decorate a crib.

The night sky here is a riot that outshines the brightest lights of Piccadilly; the stars have the intensity of jewels. So flat is the Ness that those stars that lie at the horizon touch your very feet and the moon tips the waves with silver.

The nuclear power station is a great ocean liner moored in the firmament, ablaze with light: white, yellow, ruby. Whilst round the bay the lights stretch from Folkestone to Dover. High above, jet liners from the south flash silent in the stars. On these awesome nights, reduced to silence, I walk across the Ness.

Never in my many sleepless nights have I witnessed a spectacle like this. Not the antique bells of the flocks moving up a Sardinian hillside, the barking of the dogs and the sharp cries of the shepherd boys, nor moonlit nights sailing the Aegean, nor the scented nights and fireflies of Fire Island, smashed glass star-strewn through the piers along the Hudson – nothing can quite equal this.

The orchestra has struck up the music of the spheres, the spectral dancers on the fated liner whirl you off your feet till you feel the great globe move. Light-hearted laughter. Here man has invaded the heavens; but the moon, not to be usurped, shines sickle bright, gathering in our souls.

PHARMACOPOEIA I

DAFFODIL

'Daffodowndillies' writes Thomas Hill 'is a timely flower good for shew.' Gerard in his Herbal tells us that 'Theocritus affirmeth the daffodils to grow in meadowes . . . he writeth that the fair lady Europa, entering with her nymphs into the meadowes, did gather the sweet smelling daffodils, in these verses which we may English thus:

> But when the girles here come into,
> The meadowes flouring all in sight,
> That wench with these, this wench with those,
> Trim floures, themselves did all delight;
> She with the Narcisse good in scent,
> And she with Hyacynths content.'

Daffodil bulbs were used by Galen, surgeon of the school of gladiators, to glue together great wounds and gashes; the bulbs were carried for a similar purpose in the back-packs of Roman soldiers. Perhaps this is how they first came to this country. The name daffodil, d'asphodel, is a confusion with the asphodel. They were also called Lent lily.

Daffodils 'come before the swallows dare and take the winds of March with beauty'. When I read these words they are tinged with sadness, for the seasonal nature of daffodils has been destroyed by horticulturists who nowadays force them well before Christmas. One of the joys our technological civilisation has lost is the excitement with which seasonal flowers and fruits were welcomed; the first daffodil, strawberry or cherry are now things of the past, along with the precious moment of their arrival. Even the tangerine – now a satsuma or clementine – appears de-pipped months before Christmas. I expect one day to see daffodils for sale in Berwick Street market in August, as plentiful as strawberries at Christmas. Even the humble apple has succumbed. Tough green waxy specimens have eradicated the varieties of my childhood, the pink-fleshed scented August pearmains, the laxtons and russets; only the cox seems to have survived the onslaught. Perhaps my nostalgia is out of place – now daffodils are plentiful; and mushrooms, once a luxury, are ladled out by the pound. Avocados and mangoes are commonplace. But the daffodil, if only the daffodil could come with spring again, I would eat strawberries with my Christmas pudding.

HYACINTH

The bluebell, *Hyacinthus nonscriptus,* is the hyacinth of the ancients, the flower of grief and mourning. Hyacinth, son of the king of Sparta, whose sparkling blue eyes and jet black hair enflamed Phoebus Apollo, whipped Zephyrus into a frenzy of desire; but the boy loved the sun god best, causing the wild west wind to seek a terrible revenge. One day as Hyacinth and Apollo were playing quoits Zephyrus caught a quoit in a whirlwind and smashed the boy's beautiful face, killing him. Grief-stricken, Apollo raised the purple flower from the drops of blood on which he traced the letters *ai ai,* so his anguish would forever echo through the spring.

Whenever you walk in a sunny bluebell wood, remember it is the heart of a passionate love. It is dangerous to kiss there, as the wind sighing in the branches will want to blow you and the boy apart. Your love may wilt and die as quickly as the flowers you pick, your hands will be stained with blood.

So leave the wood in peace, empty-handed. For the blue-eyed flower with its heavy fragrance only belongs to the sun.

And remember that Ovid said that Sparta was not ashamed of having produced Hyacinth, *for he is honoured there to this very day, and every year the Hyacinthian games are celebrated with festive displays, in accordance with ancient usage.*

ROSEMARY

Rosemary – *Ros marinus,* sea dew – has proved quite hardy here. My next-door neighbour has an ancient gnarled specimen – all the garden books are emphatic it hates the wind, but a more windy and exposed spot you could not find. Thomas More, who loved it, wrote, 'As for Rosemarie, I let it run all over my garden walls, not because bees love it but because it is the herb sacred to remembrance and therefore to friendship, whence a sprig of it hath a dumb language.'

The herb was part of Ophelia's bouquet: 'here's rosemary for remembrance.' Gilded and tied with ribbons it was carried at weddings; also, a sprig of it was placed in the hands of the dead. Legend has it that originally its flowers were white until the day the Virgin Mary laid out her robe to dry on some bushes, colouring them a heavenly blue.

'Where rosemary flourishes women rule': years ago on the island of Patmos, the old woman on whose roof I was sleeping washed my clothes for me, and scented them with wild rosemary from the hillside. In ancient Greece young men wore garlands of rosemary in their hair to stimulate the mind; perhaps the gathering of the Symposium was scented with it.

NARCISSUS

Narcissus is derived not from the name of the young man who met his death vainly trying to embrace his reflection in crystal water, but from the Greek *narkao* (to benumb); though of course Narcissus, benumbed by his own beauty, fell to his death embracing his shadow. Pliny says *'Narce Narcissum dictum non a fabuloso puero,'* named Narcissus from *narké,* not from the fabled boy. Socrates called the plant 'crown of the infernal gods' because the bulbs, if eaten, numbed the nervous system. Perhaps Roman soldiers carried it for this reason (rather than for its healing properties) as the American soldiers smoked marijuana in Vietnam.

PANSY

Viola tricolor, heartsease, tickle-my-fancy, love-in-idleness,
or herb trinity. The juice of it on sleeping eyelids will
make a man or woman dote upon the next live creature
they see, if you would have midsummer's dreams. A
strong tea made of the leaves will cure a broken heart;
for our pansy is strongly aphrodisiac, its name, pensée, *I
think of you.* If it leads you astray, don't worry: the herbal
says it cures the clap; for 'it is a Saturnine plant of a cold
slimy viscous nature . . . an excellent cure for venereal
disorder'.

In the old days pansies were virgin white, until Cupid
fired his arrow and turned them the colours of the rainbow. Of one thing you must beware: picking a pansy in
the first light of dawn, particularly if it is spotted with
dew, will surely bring the death of a loved one.

Was the pansy pinned to us, its velvety nineteenth
century showiness the texture of Oscar's flamboyant and

floppy clothes? As Ficino says, the gardens of Adonis are cultivated for the sake of flowers not fruits – now what about those fruits? Pansies, before you smile, are also the flower of the Trinity.

CELANDINE

Messenger of the swallow, celandine is the subject of one of the most complicated herbal remedies:

Take gallingall, cloves, cubibs, ginger, mellilote, cardamonia, maces, nutmegs, one dram. Of the juice of salandine, 8 drams. Mingle all these made in powder with the said juice and a pint of acquavit, and three pints of white wine. Put it into a stillitory of glass and the next day still it with an easy fire. This water is an excellent virtue against consumption or any other disease that proceeds from rheume, choler or fleagme.

If that seems complex, the lore of the arum is more so – Gerard informs us that:

Beares after they have lien in their dens forty days without any manner of sustenance, but what they get from licking and sucking their own feet, doe as soone as they come forth eat the herb cuckoo pint. Through the windie nature thereof the hungry gut is opened.

But the plant has more practical uses than causing bears to fart. It was used to starch the ruffs that Titian's dark young men wear – a beauty bought at the expense of the laundresses' hands, which this most pure white starch chappeth, blistereth and maketh rough and rugged and withal smarting.

VIOLETS

Gerard says of violets – that they:

Stirre up a man to that which is comely and honest; for flowres through their beauty, variety of colour, and exquisite forme, do bring to a liberal and gentle manly minde, the remembrance of honesty, comlinesse and all kinds of virtues, because it would be an unseemly and filthy thing (as a certain wise man sayeth) for him that look upon and handle faire and beautiful things to have his mind not faire, but filthy and deformed.

Culpeper adds, 'They are a fine pleasing plant of Venus, of a mild nature, no way harmful.' Pindar called Athens 'violet crowned'; garlands of violets were worn on all festive occasions, particularly on the feast of Demeter, when young men were crowned with them. In German it is still known as 'boy's herb'. Goethe always carried violet seeds on his country walks and scattered them.

LILY OF THE VALLEY

Lily of the valley was often carried in bouquets: something old, something new, something borrowed, something blue – the lily of constancy, Mary's tears, a sign of the second coming, often called 'ladder-to-heaven'. When Mary wept at the foot of the cross her tears turned into this pure white flower of humility.

The medicinal property of the Virgin's tears was considered so strong in the Middle Ages that infusions made from them were kept in gold and silver vessels, like the jewelled reliquaries that held fragments of the True Cross. Distilled in wine and ministered to the dumb it would restore speech and restore memory, clear as the bells of the flower.

SEMPERVIVUMS

In 1948 my father was posted as Commanding Officer to RAF Abingdon, near Oxford. The desolate married quarters were painted in khaki and black camouflage, the garden an uneven lawn bounded by a barbed wire fence, its only ornament a concrete 'rockery', made from an old air-raid shelter.

I returned from the watermill somewhere beyond the pub called The Rose Revived clutching a bunch of houseleeks that had been given to me by the man who lived there. They grew on his stone roof, scorched red by the wind and sun, with star-shaped rose-coloured flowers and perfectly formed miniature offshoots – each plant covered by a spider's web which trapped the dew. These flowers seemed alien exotics in his rich and vivid waterside garden, a maze of scarlet runners and blue-green cabbages over which white butterflies floated. I followed the man through this luxuriant jungle to the pig pens, keeping a cautious distance from his pet swan, which had a broken wing and hissed if I got too near (a swan, I was told, could break a man's arm, so its disability gave me some satisfaction).

The man was restoring the tumbledown buildings. He was carving a mantelpiece from a huge baulk of oak. The elder, and giant cow parsley, flag irises and ancient willows seemed poised to burst through the thick stone walls and broken windows to reclaim the muddy flagstones – an uneasy balance was struck. To keep rampant nature at bay the man carried a gun, firing at the crows in the elm trees, occasionally bringing one clattering down through the branches whilst its comrades flew higher and higher in the summer afternoon, protesting angrily.

The man, handsome and self-assured, wore an old corduroy jacket with a scarlet neckerchief knotted like a cowboy's. He smoked a pipe and walked slowly and deliberately with a limp from an old wound, which made him lean dangerously and upset my equilibrium as I walked beside him. He didn't say much. He hooked the sempervivums off the roof with his stick and presented them to me.

I carefully repeated the name *sempervivums* all the way home to Abingdon – where I planted my tongue-twisting prizes, proudly showing them off to my friends, who were not the least interested in the plants but studiously learnt their name like a litany: SEM PER VIV UM.

The houseleek under the sign of Jupiter, 'the Thunderer', protects whoever grows it against storms and lightning; its effect is so powerful that the Emperor Charlemagne ordered it grown on the roof of every home. To this day you will find it grown in the same way, surviving drought and frost, ever and always living.

FORGET-ME-NOT

Egyptian seers placed the flowers of forget-me-not on the eyes of initiates to bring dreams; the flower was sacred to Thoth, god of wisdom.

There are many stories about the name. As a child I often wondered why 'forget-me-not'? Surely it is because this beautiful blue flower is so retiring you could easily miss it.

IRIDESCENCE

My first memories are green memories. When did my fingers turn green? In the paradisiacal wilderness of the gardens at Villa Zuassa on the banks of Lago Maggiore? *The April Gift of A Hundred and One Beautiful Flowers and How to Grow Them* confirmed that at four my parents knew I was lost to green, as I walked down deep green avenues of camellias spotted with waxy carmine and white flowers. February flowers that seemed more in keeping with the hottest of midsummers.

Archaic green colours time. Passing centuries are evergreen. To mauve belongs a decade. Red explodes and consumes itself. Blue is infinite. Green clothes the earth in tranquillity, ebbs and flows with the seasons. In it is the hope of Resurrection. We feel green has more shades than any other colour, as the buds break the winter dun in the hedges. Hallucinatory sunny days.

Were Adam's eyes the green of paradise? Did they open on the vivid green of the Garden of Eden? God's green mantle. Was green the first colour of perception? After Adam bathed his eyes in green did he look at the blue sky? Or dive into the sapphire waters of the rivers of paradise? Did he fall asleep under the Tree of the Knowledge of Good and Evil? Spangled with emerald dew. Love was green then. When ancient Venus, old enough to be God's granny, furious that she had been shut out of this garden, materialised and touched Eve on the shoulder, causing her to pick the apple-green fruit that led to her downfall. Though, some have said, it was not an apple but an orange, shining like the sun at hand's reach.

She took of the fruits and ate. Then the eyes of both were open, and they knew that they were naked, and they sewed fig-leaves together and made themselves aprons.

Turfed out of the Garden of Eden for a snack by the unpleasant new God, they found themselves in a colourless world. Remember them as you buy a dozen Granny Smiths. There were few colours in the wilderness. At that time God hadn't even sent a rainbow begging for forgiveness. If he had, Adam would have returned it to the sender, for he missed the colours of Eden . . . violet and mallow (mauve), buttercup, lavender and lime.

Adam bit the fruit, and paradise, like all abandoned gardens, returned to the wild.

The hawthorn is in flower. The first elder blossoms are out; the wild pear has set fruit (my cuttings are thriving); the gorse is fading and the broom is coming into its own, the bushes skirted with gold.

The sheep's sorrel, no more than a couple of inches high, has turned the shingle a deep rust red as far as the eye can see, leaving the islands of dead brambles looking like mounds of bleached bones.

In this burnished landscape whites and greys are thrown into sharp relief. The sun beats down, though the wind has kept the butterflies in hiding; apart from the coppers I only saw a solitary white. In nooks and crannies the bird's foot trefoil, bacon-and-eggs, is beginning to flower; also the yellow rattle and treacle mustard.

On warm nights the drunken scent of the May caresses lovers under the sighing trees of Hampstead Heath. This is how I would remember it. Though others say its scent is cloying, the smell of the great plague of London.

My grandmother said it was unlucky, and should never be brought into the home. Her gardener, Moore, was married to May – which puzzled me as a child. Why should anyone have such an unlucky name? But the May could bring good luck: Wasn't the crown of England found in a thorn thicket? Here on the marsh, it was precious for building sea defences and protected by severe laws. You could lose a hand for cutting a bush. The blossom reminds me of clotted cream and the heady visions of Samuel Palmer: *White in full power from the first – deadly dark browns laid on at once.*

HB's mam says May is unlucky because the crown of thorns was made from it.

The thunderstorms we were promised never materialised though I was kept awake most of the night by my cough and temperature sweats.

Half an hour before the sun rose, in the first white light of dawn, the shingles are a ghostly bleached bone, grisaille silhouetting the grey of the shrubs and black the broom, a silent light unshattered by colour.

Dungeness bathes in a pool of clear sunlight ringed by dark purple thunder clouds. Heat shimmers off the stones – there is no wind today. Breathless the bees' lazy flight through the foxglove spires.

My blue columbine is in flower, and last year's seedlings are thriving. The columbine – aquilegia, the eagle's foot – a wild flower, has crept into my garden, one of the herbs used against the Black Death in the 14th century.

The thunder clouds move closer – a hawk hovers so high it is almost invisible. Down here on the stones blue damselflies and butterflies mate. Gold cinquefoil and bacon-and-eggs catch the last rays.

The sun is overtaken by clouds; distant boom of thunder.

Cinquefoil boiled with the fat of children made the witches' ointment, spell flower for love potions.

It's twelve – my noon flower closes shop, Jack-go-to-bed-at-noon: *It shutteth itself at twelve of the clocke and*

showeth not his face open until the next dayes sun doth make it
flower anew.

The wind got up and within minutes it was raining so hard it dripped through the roof. Soon the drive was awash.

The effect on the colours in the landscape was immediate, as if someone had brushed varnish across a dull painting. This is the first rain for over a month; the grasses sigh with relief. When the rain cleared, ravenous slugs appear in their juicy hundreds to feast on the poppies and fennel.

Who has not gazed in wonder at the snaky shimmer of petrol patterns on a puddle, thrown a stone into them and watched the colours emerge out of the ripples, or marvelled at the bright rainbow arcing momentarily in a burst of sunlight against the dark storm clouds?

The rainbow that was the covenant to Noah after the great deluge.

The strutting peacock with its acid cry, opening its tail. Shot silver and velvet, changing colour before our eyes.

The iridescent opal and moonstone, cool and mysterious, and the mother of pearl shell. Lustrous with colours, we all blew soap bubbles with rainbows into a sunny sky, which burst and disappeared as they sailed away.

Iridescence brings back childhood, shifting like a kaleidoscope.

The sad eyed chameleon
volcano grey

sits on his rock
on a thundery day
grey is his coat
and grey is his heart
grey-eyed chameleon
in deep grey thought.
A rainbow appeared
in a sudden squall
and big fat rain drops
started to fall.
'Oh rainbow colour
please wash away
the grey in my life
the grey of the day.'
Squall heard this wish
and there and then
blew him away
to the rainbow's end
where on the ground
lay a lustrous shell
rainbow bright
Mother of Pearl.
Opaline pearl

moonstone bright

petrol on puddles

and shimmering bubbles

Mother of Pearl is my delight.

Drove with Julian and Joyce across the marshes to Fairlight in the evening. It is impossible to describe the strange beauty of the landscape, particularly the Ridge and Winchelsea Beach. A great silence had descended, only broken by the twittering of swallows. Light on every blade of grass, flowers, bushes, lakes. Such contentment. The wind rushed past as Julian drove recklessly along empty roads.

For minutes on end we sat in complete silence. Little rabbits, quite unafraid, looked at us curiously as we passed by; poppies and bugloss iridescent scarlets and blues. The world like a medieval miniature or one of the unicorn tapestries in the Cloisters; the gravel path – the road to an earthly paradise, above us a wild sky with a flaming sun in bands of violet, pink, and blue.

Silvery willows, reeds like purple smoke fringing the water, splashed with orange light, cascades of wild roses, honeysuckle and pink valerian. Walls of wild sweet pea and red-hot pokers.

At moments in the deep lanes the car was swallowed in banks of lacy cowparsley – and elder.

June is the time of the garden, it is overwhelmed by sunlight and drought. I go back and forth with my watering can in garden clothes that have faded and frayed – washed-out blues and ochres. The wind grew in intensity and blew all the flowers out and the clothes line down.

At the sea's edge waves crashed, sending salty spray in veils across the Ness – not good growing weather this. Mrs Sinkins has browned off, the geranium leaves are bronzed, my loveage leans like Pisa and the wind whistles on, sending me to sleep in a storm-tossed siesta – sleeping in the afternoon is a bad sign.

In the first white light of dawn I turn white as a sheet, as I swallow the white pills to keep me alive . . . attacking the virus which is destroying my white blood cells.

The wind has blown without end for five days now, a cold north wind in June. The sea, whipped into a thousand white horses, attacks the shore. Plumes of salt blow in veils coating the windows with brine and burning the flowers. Leaves are blackened and the red poppies too, the roses are wilting, here today and gone tomorrow; but the white perennial pea is untouched. In the distance the white cliffs appear briefly before they are swallowed in the haze. I am shut in, to walk in the garden hurts my tired lungs.

The white seahorses have brought a madness here, irritable, straining at the bit. I hate white.

Then standing in the garden I notice a white flower among the blue viper's bugloss. On closer inspection it turns out to be a single albino sport. No one has ever seen one before. Is it an omen?

It seems strange that many of the flowers on the Ness grow in a small patch, sometimes singly. Maybe they were brought here in the earth and rubble used to build tracks out to the boats. There is one ivy-leaved toadflax, a square yard of scabious at the roadside, a patch of golden samphire by the Long Pits. I've found one broom rape and a small group of St. John's wort.

Other plants are much more plentiful: hawkweed, hempnettle, lesser knapweed and sheepbit; also, white clover, and haresfoot, which grows on the verge.

The range of colours in the poppies is astonishing. On the shingle at Lydd-on-Sea there is a plant that is such a deep red it might be called 'black poppy'. I'm keeping an eye on it for seed.

The groundsel is infested with the orange and black caterpillars of the burnet moth. Some plants have been devoured to skeletal remains.

Last night a walk at sundown along the beach: opium poppy, scabious, sea pea, white clover, restharrow, wild carrot, woody nightshade, evening primrose, mustard, mayweed, camomile, mallow, alkanet, daisy, larkspur, wild pansy, snapdragon, sowthistle, tufted vetch, hare's-foot, herb Robert, hop trefoil, sun spurge – all in flower.

The wind blows over the lavender and santolina which wave about like sea anemones on a coral reef, yellow and purple. The cornflowers are the most perfect blue, more iridescent than the bugloss or sage. On the kerbside red clover and dead nettle.

Breathless in the wind, picked white stones.

In the silent evening Edward, the red-haired boy next door, shoots at the flaming sun with his air rifle. The dying light turns the poppies deep scarlet, the bugloss spires a burning iridaceous purple, my sky-blue T-shirt cool against the glowing timbers of Prospect. A gentle breeze rocks the grasses silhouetted against the angry clouds. Edward fires one last shot as the sun sinks slowly behind Lydd church and disappears into the 'Bungalow for Sale'.

The coming dark smells of the sea.

Lazy high summer. The drowsy bees fall over each other in the scarlet poppies, which shed their petals by noon. Meadow browns and gatekeepers flutter wearily across the shell-pink brambles disputing the nectar with a fast bright tortoiseshell. The bees clamber hungrily up the sour green woodsage. Drifts of mauve rosebay and deep yellow ragwort studded with orange and black burnet caterpillars.

Blue damsels dart here and there, a great brown dragonfly hovers. I pick dead heads off the poppies and scatter the seeds.

Walking home I stumble across a wild fig, more bush than tree, hugging the ground. I take a slip from it, and two cuttings from the sea buckthorn. The lone fruit on the wild pear is already the size of a hen's egg.

At three I water the roses, then fall asleep in the heat, waiting for the telephone to ring me awake.

There is the suspicion of rain in the air, but a dry wind blows. The downy seeds of the willow herb float by. The black seed pods of the broom split with a crackling sound.

At the end of the garden the sloes are turning purple, and the blackberries are ripe. My wild pear tree wilts in the drought, and the nettles are dead and rattle in the wind.

By the lake a large grass snake curves silently across our path through the withered grass. Swans stand forlorn on barren stony islands that have emerged from the water.

Everything is waiting for rain: the great burdock, purple with bloom, flags like a thirsty dog; the grey moss crumbles like ash under my feet. Only the yellow ragwort, bright with tortoiseshell butterflies, is happy with this long summer; while an angry cloud of smoke from the burning fields hangs in the bare blue sky.

I never saw the verdigris green charioteer of Delphi, a statue I imagined to be the most beautiful in the world. When I was eighteen I hitch-hiked there with some friends and was left a mile or two down the mountain road. Walking in the dark, we heard a small stream gurgling under a bridge and decided to stop and set up camp. We had been hiking since early morning, tired and dusty, with no money for a hotel or a youth hostel. We fell into a deep sleep a few yards from the road.

At dawn, we discovered ourselves in a cleft in the mountain. A chasm in which fig trees grew, watered by a crystal spring that sprang from the rock. We took off our clothes and washed them, hanging them to dry on the branches. Then bathed and shaved in the icy water, and sat in the warming sunlight waiting for our clothes to dry. At about seven, a rather angry visitor appeared, said something we couldn't understand and left scowling. Half an hour later, the silence was shattered by two police vans, from which a dozen or so policemen piled out, shouting. Confusion reigned as we couldn't understand a word they were saying. They furiously kicked our rucksacks, and threw our clothes in the dust, trampling on them. In our swimming pants we were very vulnerable.

David, who had climbed a rock face to get a clearer view of two eagles that circled in the updraft high above us, fell from his perch on the cliff face, and was saved from severe injury or even death by some rusty barbed wire at the bottom of the cliff which broke his fall. He lay bleeding and unconscious in a tangle of wire. The atmosphere changed, and we were bundled into the van, with the police siren blaring down to the hospital in Amphissa. There we were told never to return to Delphi.

We stayed in Amphissa several days while David recovered, his wounds painted scarlet with iodine. We learned that we had committed sacrilege. We had swum in the sacred well of Apollo, where the Pythian Priestess spoke her oracle.

I have always believed that this was my real baptism for the well brought the gift of dreams, prophecy. The ancients believed it was the fount of poetry. It was here they came for inspiration.

What has happened to me under these awesome skies? Here the preoccupations of a film world bounded by Soho seem ridiculous. Walking into Working Tide or Basilisk, the offices seem so cramped, so steeped in gloom all this glorious summer.

Behind the facade my life is at sixes and sevens. I water the roses and wonder whether I will see them bloom. I plant my herbal garden as a panacea, read up on all the aches and pains that plants will cure – and know they are not going to help. The garden as pharmacopoeia has failed.

Yet there is a thrill in watching the plants spring up that gives me hope.

Even so, I find myself unable to record the disaster that has befallen some of my friends, particularly dear Howard, who I miss more than imagination.

He wanders into my mind – as he wandered out of a stormy night eighteen months ago.

The foghorn boomed through the night in a dense mist, which left the garden sparkling with dewy spiders' webs. As the sun came up the mist glowed an iridescent white. For an hour you could see only a few yards, though it quickly cleared, leaving the garden with a myriad diamond drops, the poppies with their hairy leaves were strings of pearls. At seven one of the washed mauve opium poppies opened.

I sat by the front door wafted by the clove-scented pinks, it is an idyll: *et in Arcadia ego*. I am so in love with the place please God I see another year.

Cloudy, with a warm dry wind. It had hardly rained here, which surprised me, as the deluge in London felt as if it must have covered the whole country. More damaging than the drought is the strong wind, as it dries out the plants.

With the hosepipe ban the view has become a desert, everything left to chance and the isobars. The sloe bushes are heavy with purple fruit a full six weeks in advance of last year – we picked them in early October. The rosemary bushes are dying, and most of the flowers are over – the geraniums and marigolds, scarlets and reds. The brave bugloss is at a finish. Picked up the dead flower heads of the sempervivum and night scented stock, trimmed lavender flowers. Reponed seedlings of foxglove and great mullein; also sea buckthorn and the wild fig.

To prove there was a life after
A man had himself buried six feet under
In a lead-lined coffin, holding a fig.

He said, 'If a life after exists, the fig will grow.'
The fig grew. That's quite certain.
As a child I ate the figs of eternal life;
They were unripe and gave me colic.

Dungeness might seem the least hospitable environment for a fig tree to take root. Cut back by biting winter easterlies it is a mere couple of feet high, dwarfed but thriving. Sycamore and oak have established themselves in the same way.

A band of rain blew over at dawn. Warm sunny day which clouded over.

Before the sun disappeared we filmed David out on the shore amongst the fishing boats, lying in huge coils of rope. Then, as film was running low, we made a trip to Rye; but by the time we returned the sun was lost.

A sullen evening: parched flowers dying, menacing clouds mounting above burning stubble, ploughed fields drained of life – the only movement, the silvery grey leaves of the willows along the drainage canals.

Julian swung the car along the empty roads like a rally driver, in silence.

Dark by 8:30. Evenings drawing in.

I sat and wrote this poem, the bright sunlight through the window hurting my eyes.

No dragons will spring from these circles.
These stones will not dance or clap hands at the solstice.
Beached on the shingle,
They lock up their memories,
Upright as sentinels
In the dry grass.
Rolled by the sea down the centuries
They wait the great Tide
That shall come a second time
Recalling them to the depths
Where the salt sea will unlock their silence.
Then they'll talk of their time here
To strange creatures,
Telling them how the postman came up
The path with your letter,

How I couldn't conceal my happiness,

And walked backwards and forwards in the garden,

skipping.

How, when you came, we set off under a full moon,

To watch the patient fishermen,

And then turned home,

Throwing handfuls of pebbles

In showers of sparks

Under the starlit sky.

Of your face, lit by the beam from the lighthouse,

Every ten seconds,

A smile,

A little frown,

Green eyes,

A wink.

Planted out santolinas and fig tree cuttings.

Sat in the deck chair and watched the sun set and a full moon climb over the lighthouse through bands of iridescent cloud.

The stones reflect the great circle of the moon. They can hear me singing in the kitchen.

Brought in seeds of alexanders, burdock, hawkbit and yellow horned poppy. Replanted seedlings of the poppy and ivy-leaved toadflax; also the periwinkle from Phoenix House.

Everything dry as a bone. White groundsel seeds like pearls in a desert. Teasel, thistles, and the burdocks scorched and dying – nothing left for the rain to save. Even the willows rattle with drought.

A cool northerly brought the skies back. Fast-moving low cloud over bright silver with shafts of light. The sea running high, white capped; shimmering dead grasses. The summer's back broken.

The sun has picked out the white cliffs, like a vast iceberg in a dark blue-grey sea. The crow followed me out to the Long Pits and saw off the small dog of a couple of surprised hikers. Took cuttings of the dog roses, slips of yarrow; scattered seed of the white poppy from the seashore at Greatstone. Built windchimes from metal rods and two baulks of timber from the beach.

Just before sunset a rainbow glowed across a dark sea offset by violet pink cumulonimbus clouds.

PHARMACOPOEIA II

POPPY

Nearly all the flowers that grow so abundantly on our shingle find a place in folklore or the herbals.

The petals of the red poppy were once collected on sunny days and made into a syrup; while the seeds are scattered over bread – the Romans mixed them with honey and ate them like jam.

The poppy is rarer than it once was. Gerard wrote *The fields are garnished and overspread with these wild poppies.*

Scarlet Poppies
This is a poppy
A flower of cornfield and wasteland
Bloody red
Sepals two
Soon falling
Petals four
Stamens many
Stigma rayed

Many seeded

For sprinkling on bread

The staff of life

Woven in wreaths

In memory of the dead

Bringer of dreams

And sweet forgetfulness

FOXGLOVE

I always thought of foxglove as a flower of the woods – deep in the shade, beloved of the bumble bee and little people. But the foxgloves of the Ness are a quite different breed. Strident purple in the yellow broom, they stand exposed to wind and blistering sunshine, as rigid as guardsmen on parade.

There they are at the edge of the lakeside, standing to attention, making a splash – no blushing violets these, and not in ones or twos but hundreds, proud regiments marching in the summer, with clash of cymbals and rolling drums. Here comes June. Glorious, colourful June.

The foxglove, Digitalis purpurea, folksglove, or fairyglove – whose speckles and freckles are the marks of elves' fingers, is also called dead man's fingers. It contains the poison Digitalis, first used by a Dr Withering in the 18th century to cure heart disease. Foxglove is hardly mentioned in older herbals – Gerard says, it has no use in medicine, being hot and dry and bitter. The 'glove' comes from the Anglo-Saxon for a string of bells, 'gleow'.

DILL

Dill, like its cousin fennel, has a strong sweet taste used in pickling and with vegetables. The seeds have a soporific effect and were eaten in church to dull the agony of listening to sermons. The name of the herb is derived from the Anglo-Saxon dilla, to lull. Dill sent the witches flying.

There with her vervain and her dill
That hindereth witches of their will
A scarewitch stuffed with dill

DOG ROSE

In that garden be floures of hewe,
The gelofir gent that she well knew,
The flower de luce she did on rewe
And said, 'The white rose is most true
The garden to rule by rightwis lawe'
The lily-white rose me thought I sawe
And ever she sang . . .

This medieval poem, which probably describes *Rosa alba* – the white rose of York – could equally describe the dog rose, *Rosa canina,* of the hedgerow. Pliny says it grew so plentifully here that this island was named Albion.

The dog rose can live as long as the yew: there is one old bush in Hildesheim Cathedral said to have been planted by Charlemagne.

BUGLOSS

Of bugloss Culpeper says

*It is a gallant herb of the sun, it is a pity it is no more use
than it is. The gentlewomen of France do paint their faces
with these roots, it is said.*

Two to three foot high, it is covered with clear blue
flowers, and of all the plants of the Ness is the brightest:

*Viper's bugloss has its stalkes all to be speckled like a snake
or viper, and is a most singular remedy against poison and
the sting of scorpions. – Cole's, Art Of Simples – The water
distilled in glasses and the roote taken itself is good against
the passions and tremblings of the heart, as also against
swoonings, sadness, and melancholy.*

YARROW

In the garden the yarrow is blooming – *Herba militaris*, achillea, a wound herb used to staunch blood. Wound-wort, knight's milfoil, nosebleed, staunch grass, bloodwort, sanguinary – also known as devil's plaything – yarrow was brushed over a victim as the dark one cast a spell.

GREAT MULLEIN

The great mullein was the herb that Ulysses used as a protection against Circe's enchantment. These flowers were used by Romans to dye hair yellow: *The golden floweres of mullen stiped in lye causeth the heare to war yellow being washed withal.*

The plant had many uses: it drew splinters, cured earache; dipped in wax, it was used as a taper – *the whole toppe with its pleasant yellow flowers sheweth like to a wax candle or taper cunningly wrought.* Verbascum *is of the latines called candelaria because the elder age used the stalkes dipped in suet to burne wether at funerals or otherwise.*

Cole in his *Adam and Eve* writes: *The husbandmen of Kent do give it to their cattle against the cough of the lungs.* It was called 'clown's lungwort'.

AGRIMONY

If it be leyd under a man's heed
he shall sleepen as he wer deed
he shall never drede ne wakyn
till fro under his heed it be takyn.

The yellow flowers of Agrimonia eupatoria are named after Mithridates Eupator, a king who brewed herbal remedies. It is known colloquially as 'church steeples' and yields a bright yellow dye. 'A decoction of the leaves,' says Gerard, 'is good for them with naughty livers.' 'A herb of princely authority,' says Pliny.

MUGWORT

The ragwort *Artemisia vulgaris* was used once as a substitute for tea or to flavour drinks. Placed between linen its dried branches warded off moths. *Cingulum Sancti Johannis* was worn by John the Baptist as a girdle in the wilderness; it also preserved the traveller from fatigue and sunstroke, pixies, elves, and wild beasts. Make a charm of it and wear it on St John's Eve for protection against the evil eye.

This tall silvery herb grows deep green by the wayside despite the drought. Culpeper says: *A very slight infusion is excellent for all disorders of the stomach, prevents sickness after meals, and creates an appetite, but if made too strong disgusts the taste.*

I'm going to wear a crown of the wort tonight, not wait for St John's Eve. And put a leaf in my shoe, as this will enable me to walk 40 miles before midday without getting tired.

CROCUS

The crocus produced the best yellow for the illuminated manuscripts of the Middle Ages – many of the plants that grow on the Ness once produced dyes. The finest blue 'turnsole' was made from the juice of elderberries – sap green from the berries of the buckthorn, and a bright green from the juice of the flag iris.

Other colours – vermillion, cobalt, and bright lapis blue – were mineral. Antonello da Messina's little study of St Jerome in a monastery scriptorium – with a dazzling postage stamp sized landscape through an open window – shows the calm and tranquil rooms in which these manuscripts were prepared.

The crocus that was used as a dye was the saffron crocus – Arabic Z à Faran, the yellow one. Thomas Smith, Edward III's counsellor, brought it secretly from the Holy Land in 1330. The dye was exquisitely expensive: 4,320 flowers were required to produce one ounce of saffron. John the Gardener wrote:

They should be set in the month of September, three days before St Mary Day, Nativity, or the next week thereafter; so must it be with a dibble you shall set him, that the dibble before be blunt and great. Three hands deep they must set be.

Petals of the saffron crocus were strewn across Jupiter's marriage bed; it dyed wedding robes and the robes of monks. Gerard says saffron brought those dying of the plague back from the deathbed.

PARADISE

The summer is over. The corn harvested. The fields are ploughed. The ploughman wears chocolate brown corduroy. Brown is the colour of riches. The man who owns acres is a rich man, both in pocket and hopefully in soul. For the soul is deep . . . a peaceful brown. However much you possess in life, even if your land stretches beyond the horizon, in death you will end up with six foot.

The woods and hedgerows turn the innumerable shades of brown from yellow to red. I ran back and forth in the dying light of October; catching the gold-brown leaves as they fell from the chestnut trees before they touched the earth and were swept up into the bonfire. Each leaf caught in the air brought you a lucky day. They floated slowly in spirals, as we threw sticks for the conkers, which we warmed in the oven till they were as hard as stone, then fought each other bruising our knuckles.

★

Brown is a slow colour. It takes its time. It is the colour of winter. It is also a colour of hope, for we know it will not be blanketed by icy snow for ever.

The sisters of Perpetual Indulgence all here for the anniversary of my sainting, with a congregation of sixty. We built the altar with a large teddy bear, a first birthday cake and a bubble bath duck. Simon Sebastian looking tremendous with a silver nose piercing, which looks like an upturned Dali moustache. I was given a very beautiful sculpture made from a Portuguese sardine tin – of an articulated figure like Ned Kelly. The sun shone and it was a good deal warmer than last year. My good deeds were read out and my gorgeous nose praised – it was all very affecting. I know I'm not to take this too seriously but my feelings were rather emotional. What miracles have taken place? I think the best is that we are all still here.

It rained very hard during the night; dawn came with little light, grey and suddenly cold. Dungeness quiet and deserted except for the whine of a plane somewhere above the clouds and the cries of seagulls at the sea's edge. A migraine hovered over my left eye but after a bath and breakfast of toast and sweet grapefruit it retreated. I tied up the pyramids which protect the gorse from the rabbits. Why should rabbits take such a liking to my spiky cuttings? There is little out now, just nasturtiums and Californian poppies, the blue-green sea cabbages are beginning to shed leaves and the scarlet hips on the roses have turned a deeper red.

Along the beach I find more metal chains to fix the sempervivums on the roof. It is very desolate: a pile of railway sleepers marks the passage of a boat into the water, but the boat is nowhere to be seen in the grey mists that hug the water.

How did my friends cross the cobalt river, with what did they pay the ferryman? As they set out for the indigo shore under this jet-black sky – some died on their feet with a backward glance. Did they see Death with the hell hounds pulling a dark chariot, bruised blue-black, growing dark in the absence of light, did they hear the blast of trumpets?

David ran home panicked on the train from Waterloo, brought back exhausted and unconscious to die that night. Terry who mumbled incoherently into his incontinent tears. Others faded like flowers cut by the scythe of the Blue Bearded Reaper, parched as the waters of life receded. Howard turned slowly to stone, petrified day by day, his mind imprisoned in a concrete fortress until all we could hear were his groans on the telephone circling the globe.

A wild storm blew in during the night, rattling the corrugated roof, buffeting the house in fits and starts, a high sea running down the channel with a huge tanker sending up plumes of white spray like a rock . . . I'm glad I'm awake and it's light – at night I'm prey to fears and can never sleep with a gale blowing after the hurricane that huffed and puffed like the big bad wolf at the door.

The broom is burnt black with the salt, as are the marigolds, even the red hips are falling from the dog rose, the sea kale are dying back, but the artichoke looks set to defy the winter . . .

I live in a twilight here from day to day, neither earth nor heaven, the pain circles month after month breaking you down.

HB says he would give anything to give me a day free from this and says if we could swap bodies, and I promised to look after his, he would let me borrow it, but the reality of a sunny day might drive me insane and enduring this would kill him.

At first, people thought I was building a garden for magical purposes – a white witch out to get the nuclear power station. It did have magic – the magic of surprise, the treasure hunt. A garden is a treasure hunt, the plants the paperchase.

I invest my stones with the power of those at Avebury. I have read all the mystical books about ley-lines and circles – I built the circles with this behind my mind. The circles make the garden perfect – in winter they take over from the flowers. There was magic and hard work in finding the coloured stones for the front: white, difficult; grey, less so; red, very rare.

Some of the flints are over a foot high: these are the central hub; some are grey, a very few white and a warm brown, the others mottled white and grey. The bricks, washed smooth by the tide, bring a jolly flash of red.

★

The garden is full of metal: rusty metal corkscrew clumps, anchors from the beach, twisted metal, an old table-top with a hole for the umbrella, an old window, chains which form circles round the plants. All this disappears in the burgeoning spring. The twisted grimace of the wartime mines, an arch, a hook, a plummet, a line, a shellcase – warlike once; a chain that has rusted to form a snake by the front door, more chimes made of triangles of rusty iron; all this – and the float that looks like an exotic fruit – introduces a warm brown which contrasts nicely with the shingle.

Red. Prime colour. Red of my childhood. Blue and green were always there in the sky and woodland unnoticed. Red first shouted at me from a bed of pelargoniums in the courtyard of Villa Zuassa. I was four. This red had no boundary, was not contained. These red flowers stretched to the horizon.

Red protects itself. No colour is as territorial. It stakes a claim, is on the alert against the spectrum.

Red adapts the eye for the dark. Infra-red.

In the old garden red had a smell, as I brushed the leaves of the zonal pelargonium, scarlet filled my nostrils. I have called the plant formal pelargonium rather than geranium, as geranium conjures a dirty pink. The scarlet of Paul Crampel is the perfect scarlet. The scarlet of flower beds; civic, municipal, public red, reflected in the jolly red buses that bring a touch of joy to the dank grey streets.

★

I'm four again. Zonal pelargoniums light up my eyes. There I am picking huge bunches of them in the mind's eye of Dad's movie.

I am sitting here writing this in a bright red T-shirt from Marks and Spencer. I shut my eyes. In the dark, I can remember the red, but I cannot see it.

My red pelargoniums, the colour of flaming June, have never died. Each autumn I take cuttings, and though they are conned to a few flowerpots, when I look at them I see the past. Other colours change. The grass is not the green of my youth. Nor the blue of the Italian sky. They are in flux. But the red is constant. In the evolution of colour red stops.

Childhood flowers, dew-bowed peonies, dark red, along the paths at Curry Malet. The ivy stencil veins of the crocus purple and white, stamens yellow for painting. The buddleia covered with tortoiseshell butterflies, peacock and humming-bird hawks. Purple mulberry – should you eat it? Scarlet geraniums, jasmine, scent of the night stock, *Aloe variegata,* the camellia – exotic in February; wisteria on old stone walls, wallflowers – wild and draught-defying – balsam poplars brown purple; celandine with yellow brimstone flashing across the lawn.

Dried chincherinchees sent across the world to bloom at Christmas. Güta, the Christmas tree ablaze with candles. Petunias, stock, lupins in school gardens – mysterious spires. Privet and lime. Moth-hunting in the bathroom deep in the night: ermine and emerald. Drinkers; mysterious hawk moths; the multicoloured lackey; puss moth caterpillars on the cliffside with forked devil's tails; goat moths thick as your finger; all the wild meadows now long vanished.

Syringa in the vases. A cream white rose climbing through the old apples. Gathering worts in Holford. The great monastic poplars by the stream.

At Kilve: fossils grey on the muddy reefs of the beach. The wind, the great yew; bulrushes in the moat; tall Lombardy poplars.

Cowparsley peashooters, ivy ammunition, smell of cowparsley. Stolen carrots and radish. Cress in the bathroom. Eating the ripening corn in a den carved in the fields. Clove-scented white ragged pinks along the borders. Shy aquilegia, wild in the woods. Walking on air high above in the trees.

My cacti gardens. Beans for salting: scarlet, french and broad. Never a cauliflower. Spinach, radish and Tom Thumb lettuce.

All this I remember at 12:30 after a night sweat.

Restless night. Fell asleep at dawn as the sun cast a rosy glow into this room. Across the marshes a full moon, white in a pale blue sky.

My fever has brought a deep, almost comforting lethargy. Spring remarked yesterday that I was unusually calm – it seems ridiculous to worry.

Four years ago I wouldn't have thought twice about it, just made a trip to the doctor and come away with a prescription. Now I will myself to get better without the aid of antibiotics, feel almost ashamed of pottering off to the Kobler centre to take up valuable time.

I refuse to believe in my mortality, or the statistics which hedge the modern world about like the briar that walled in the sleeping princess. I have conducted my whole life without fitting in, so why should I panic now and fit into statistics?

When the doctor first told me I was HIV positive,

I think she was more upset than me. It didn't sink in at first – that took weeks. I thought: this is not true, then I realised the enormity. I had been pushed into yet another corner, this time for keeps. It quickly became a way of life. When the sun shone it became unbearable. I didn't say anything, I had decided to be stoic.

This was a chance to be grown-up. Though I thought I ought to be crying. I walked down Charing Cross Road in the sunlight, everyone was so blissfully unaware. The sun is still shining.

The perception that knowing you're dying makes you feel more alive is an error. I'm less alive. There's less life to lead. I can't give 100% attention to anything – part of me is thinking about my health.

Prospect Cottage is the last of a long line of 'escape houses' I started building as a child at the end of the garden: grass houses of fragrant mowings that slowly turned brown and sour; sandcastles; a turf hut, hardly big enough to turn around in; another of scrap metal and twigs, marooned on ice-flooded fields – stomping across brittle ice.

Ice flowers left out overnight in glasses, chrysanthemums suspended in frozen water – pink with cold.

I walk in this garden

Holding the hands of dead friends

Old age came quickly for my frosted generation

Cold, cold, cold they died so silently

Did the forgotten generations scream?

Or go full of resignation

Quietly protesting innocence

Cold, cold, cold they died so silently

Linked hands at four AM

Deep under the city you slept on

Never heard the sweet flesh song

Cold, cold, cold they died so silently

I have no words

My shaking hand

Cannot express my fury

Sadness is all I have,
Cold, cold, cold they died so silently

Matthew fucked Mark fucked Luke fucked John
Who lay in the bed that I lie on
Touch fingers again as you sing this song
Cold, cold, cold they died so silently

My gilly flowers, roses, violets blue
Sweet garden of vanished pleasures
Please come back next year
Cold, cold, cold I die so silently

Goodnight boys,
Goodnight Johnny,
Goodnight,
Goodnight.

A thin winter sun. My head aches at the frontier of my vision, my stomach churns, turns, a dull thud in the eye, my neck irritated by a rash I have had since I first fell ill.

Am I happy? Yes. Continuously entertained by HB and his sad long face as the washing machine dies in the darkened kitchen.

Derek Ball cooked one of his piping hot Dungeness fish stews. His friends Tim and Tod lit the guy they had built: a Minoan snake goddess in the image of Imelda Marcos carrying a pair of golden shoes – with a conical dress of driftwood and floral crimplene wired together with fireworks, high-waisted with a belt of gold streamers and breasts of hangers. A small face painted on a paper plate – delicate as the moon, with an enigmatic smile. Arms outstretched, she stood ten feet tall and burnt like a torch.

Derek's cat Spyder chased sparks in the dark. The lighthouse flashed over the Channel and the twinkling lights of fishing boats. Sheet lightning illuminated distant thunder clouds. The stars shone bright and Maria Callas blasted out Puccini arias in the dark. Tod and Tim stoked the flames in long black highwaymen's coats.

Will my voice echo till time ends? Will it journey forever into the void?

Is black hopeless? Doesn't every dark thundercloud have a silver lining? In black lies the possibility of hope.

The universal sleep is hugged by black. A comfortable, warm black. This is no cold black, it is against this black that the rainbow shines like the stars.

Black is boundless, the imagination races in the dark. Vivid dreams careering through the night. Goya's bats with goblin faces chuckle in the dark.

In the black coal fire lives the spirit of storytelling. Flickering blue and scarlet flames. It was around the fire at night that men and women told their stories in the pitchy black.

Prospect Cottage has four rooms. I call this room the Spring room; it is my writing room and bedroom, 12ft by 10 of polished tongue and groove with a single window facing the sea. In front of the window is my desk: a simple 18th century elm table. On it is a reading lamp of tarnished copper, two pewter mugs full of stamps, loose change, paperclips, several bottles of ink, and pens, envelopes, scraps of paper on which to make notes for this diary, an iron spittoon used as an ashtray; in the centre a lead tobacco box in the shape of a little Victorian cottage, in which I keep my chequebook and money.

To the left and right against the wall are two Red Cross medicine chests from an army surplus store; here I keep my clothes. A large oak chest dominates the room: it has 15th century panels carved with decorative ogee arches, perhaps once part of a rood screen. I keep my bedding in it. Next to it is a teak and khaki canvas campaign chair. By the desk is a small chair with a rush seat carved with two Maltese crosses.

On three walls are three paintings:

Night Life
The scarlet and black painting of fire, done in 1980.
Sleep has the House
A driftwood and glass construction with a carved figure, 21 December 1987.
Glittering Astronaut
By John Maybury.

In the four corners of the room are driftwood staffs crowned with garlands of stone and polished bone; on one of these sits my pixie Twinkle-in the-eye. Purple velvet curtains shut out the winter stars.

A still, frosty morning – sun bright on the glittering shingle, not a cloud in the sky and very cold. Well wrapped I walked to the beach.

I love the mornings here – up with the sunshine, cups of coffee, steaming porridge and toast. The quiet is overwhelming after the snarling traffic of the Charing Cross Road.

Now the flowers are dead; the multicoloured flints, and the bright red bricks ground by the waves give it a friendly appearance.

It isn't a gloomy garden, its circles and squares have humour – a fairy ring for troglodytic pixies – the stones a notation for long-forgotten music, an ancestral round to which I add a few more notes each morning.

By sundown yesterday a new window was opened up in the kitchen wall. I ate my supper facing the nuclear power station – ablaze with light under a star-filled sky and mandarin moon. A twentieth century Babylon, great glittering liner beached in the wilderness.

A new ladder to the fishing loft is also in place, which has made the house asymmetrical. It has made the climb a leisurely affair: no more balancing on wobbly ladders. I painted it with sticky black tar varnish – tar itself is impossible to find since the coke fired gas plants closed down.

I don't know whether to laugh or cry for the unseasonable warmth and sunshine of the last four days. The thrift outside the front door is at sixes and sevens and has put out bright pink flowers. In spite of a weather forecast that foretold rain it is warm and sunny again. I walked along the beach gathering stones with holes and returned to thread them into a necklace.

*

As the sun went down the rain set in. I am surprised how happy I have been with my own company these last few weeks – by now I should be itching to get back to London. But I'm happy here, brewing a scatterbrained mix of soups and porridge.

I'm walking along the beach in a howling gale –

Another year is passing

In the roaring waters

I hear the voices of dead friends

Love is life that lasts forever.

My heart's memory turns to you

David. Howard. Graham. Terry. Paul . . .

But what if this present

Were the world's last night?

In the setting sun your love fades

Dies in the moonlight

Fails to rise

Thrice denied by cock crow

In the dawn's first light.

I find it mysterious that all the years that have passed should lead to Prospect Cottage – perhaps it is the tin roof which reminds me of the Nissen huts of an RAF childhood in its forties, so thrifty and far distant; maybe it is the flower bed which runs in front of the house – it has the same lumps of concrete from some long-demolished fortification as those in Abingdon and Kidlington; or the stoves which roar in the wind; or maybe the name Prospect.

Today there is solitude, a half-hour has elapsed without a car passing and the phone is silent, and though it's cold I'm well wrapped up in my grey sweater and an old corduroy jacket – as worn as a moss-grown wall. I feel higgledy-piggledy. No appetite today.

A view of boats fuzzed by the dismal rain that patters on the metal roof. The smallest money spider is building a web on the desk light, so fine that my breath swings it back and forth. It's possible to be alone here.

My garden is a memorial, each circular bed and dial a true lover's knot – planted with lavender, helichrysum and santolina.

Santolina, under the dominion of Mercury resisteth poison, putrefaction, and heals the bites of venomous beasts. Whilst a sprig of lavender held in the hand or placed under the pillow enables you to see ghosts, travel to the land of the dead.

While Peter digs holes for the hellebores we find the first snowdrops peeping through the pinks, which have covered large areas of the front beds, more bright marigolds and few purple crocus in bloom. In spite of the wind and cold there are a few buds breaking on the elder, and the poppies and cornflowers have doubled in size since Christmas.

The first splatter of rain sparkles the windows, I was going to clean them but a wave of lethargy kept me from wandering around the garden. There is a gale blowing, though it is not cold – gales disturb my equilibrium.

I've put some plants out and placed the Appledore crucifix under the Florentine trumpet. The garden looks a January delight; in spite of the gales everything is ready to contend with the summer, which besets the flowers more than the cold and dark.

All day long the sun tried to break through the clouds, twice it started to rain and then thought better of it. I could feel the cold on my back as I worked in the garden planting cistus, teucrium and two new iris. Busy as a lark, industrious as a bumble bee – I saw a large one in my daffodils. HB hates daffs, says they look vulgar. Here they stand surreal in the shingle, quite out of place.

The grape hyacinth loves the shingle and each year increases itself by bounds. They are sturdy, defy the salt winds and last for months, some have been out for weeks, others are bursting into bloom.

The sea kale have grown inches in the last week, the deep inky purple has a touch of green in it, the same colour as the wallflower buds. The sea, which was roaring rough yesterday, is a calm, milky turquoise. The seagulls are squabbling with the crows, fishermen are repairing the boat that was stove in in the storm. The bees, bright-yellow with gorse-pollen, are blown off course and crawl around the hive waiting for a lull in the gusts.

Brian had painted the house a shiny black with tar varnish, he is to restore Prospect Cottage – I'm having new windows and a diamond door, with leaded 'Love is life that lasts for ever'.

Prospect ablaze with wallflowers, although it was raining and my nose was running with cold I could just smell them. The garden has leapt away, there are tulips, the first cornflower, enormous flower heads on the artichokes, scarlet anemones and the last grape hyacinths. There are buds on the valerian and the borage is out.

It was a day of moving and pottering.

SOURCES

Modern Nature (MN); *Smiling in Slow Motion* (SISM); *Chroma* (CH); *Derek Jarman's Garden* (DJG)

MN, 13/02/1989

Gorse and Gold

MN, 24/02/1989; MN 25/02/1989

MN 01/01/1989

MN 28/02/1989

CHROMA pg. 51

MN 03/02/1989; 20/05/1989

MN 07/03/1989

MN 21/03/1989

MN 22/03/1989

MN 24/03/1989

DJG pg. 12

SISM 25/04/1993

MN 05/04/1989

MN 07/04/1989

MN 07/03/1989

MN 08/04/1989

Iridescence

CHROMA pg. 50

CHROMA pg. 47

MN 13/05/1989

MN 24/05/1989

MN 03/06/1989

CHROMA pg. 116

MN 10/06/1989

MN 16/06/1991

CHROMA pg. 15

MN 02/07/1989

MN 04/07/1990

MN 06/07/1990

MN 10/07/1989

MN 31/07/1989

CHROMA pg. 55

MN 11/11/1989;

SISM 07/06/1992

MN 12/08/1989; 14/08/1989

MN 15/08/1989

MN 27/08/1989

Paradise

CHROMA pg. 62

SISM 12/09/1992

SISM 03/10/1992

CHROMA pg. 91

SISM 25/10/1992

DJG Pg. 47

CHROMA pg. 24-5

MN 04/1990

MN 16/09/1989

MN 04/1990

MN 27/04/1989

SISM 23/09/1992

MN 04/11/1989

CHROMA pp. 109-110

MN 08/03/1989

MN 06/11/1989

MN 07/11/1989

CHROMA pg. 85

MN 30/03/1992

MN 15/04/1989

SISM 17/01/1993

SISM 26/03/1992

SISM 24/04/1993